Other Echoes

*Wendy —
I feel like I've known
you forever! your soul
is so bright & beautiful.
I am blessed to have you
in my life —
All my love —
Ren
Dec. 03*

by
Ren Matney

ISBN: 0-9715555-0-8

Printed in the United States by:
Morris Publishing
3212 East Highway 30
Kearney, NE 68847
1-800-650-7888

This book is for Mark and Lloyd.
I love you.

Dedicated to the memory of

Perry Matney,
(I miss you. I'll always watch the snow for your return)

Wayne Deans,
(We are forever riding our bikes together)

Arley Forcht,
(I'm home now. Please come in.)

and

Jose Montoya.
(I see you in something new each day. You are Peace.)

I will always remember each one of you.

Acknowledgments:

To each and everyone who helped Mark and Lloyd get through their illnesses from Doctors and Nurses to Friends and Family. Especially Kevin and Meri Bender for everything, to Carole Matney for flying our baby home and Sarah Lesnak for being our surprise "Guardian Angel" during "The Phoeni-x Files." We love you.

Mirae Grant for whom I didn't know when the work had begun and yet without knowing wouldn't have this work finished. Your inspiration and love is cherished beyond all measure. "You are always needed"

All of my love: Marlene and Doyal Schell, Dena DeCastro, Ron Frasier, Jim Curtin, Tom Johnson and Onnolee Schell.

Special Thanks to Linda Blair for her tireless hard work for the animals. I have spent my life loving her celebrity and hoped one day to meet her and share our bond with loving animals like we do. I have always held her up as one of my true heroes. Her actions are an inspiration to me and now I am proud and honored to call her my friend. From her I learned dreams do come true and can even be better than you ever expected. Together we, and countless others are fighting to save the animals from lives of pain and torture. Please visit www.thealternet.com for info. and/or contact me personally at otherechoes@cs.com to see what you can do to help save the animals. Plus get Linda's book "Going Vegan!" it will change your life.

Finally to Mark and Lloyd. I am the luckiest person because I get to spend this lifetime with you. You both show me so much love on a daily basis that I couldn't imagine being without you. This work began when I thought I was going to lose you and it ended with getting the chance to see you both reclaim your lives. I am so proud of you for dealing with being sick with smiles on your faces. Each of you taught me so much and I love you both most!

Preface

Within each one of us is the beautiful language of poetry and verse, handed down through the times of growth from generations of our elders to give us a calm and reassuring voice. Here it sits, awaiting the reading that assures each thought that it has a purpose and has not been put onto paper, thus has been acknowledged and created, just to be forgotten. Nothing should ever feel forgotten. Ever.

I started to write verse the moment I started to use words as a form of communication. I didn't start to write it down until years later when I needed a release from the troubling circumstances I was facing on my journey at that time. I had family going through life-threatening illnesses, and my future seemed lonely. I felt like I was going to be left with questions of "Why?" and "What should I have been able to do?" for their survival. I wrote to think. I wrote to feel. I may have even written to pray. I am not a religious man this time around. I am however, very spiritually empathic and throughout this work you'll see me ask for help. As I know you have before. As I know we all will again one day.

There is an old superstition about St. Elmo's Fire. It is a name most commonly given by sailors to the electrical light discharged during storms. Depending on the circumstances surrounding the discharge, often dismissed as lightning, it is said to give a warning of good or bad luck to come. Because the light usually comes near the end of the worst part of the storm, it can give some sailors a good feeling, that the worst is over, and better, calmer times are to come. I think about this St. Elmo's Fire when I look back over this piece of work. I was really scared and searching during the writing of this poetry, and yet, when I read it now, I know that deep down inside I knew that most of these thoughts were my own St. Elmo's Fire.

My clue that the times, no matter how bad they seem, will always get better. Funny thing is that I don't remember writing most of it. Something inside my head just takes over and out it comes, usually in only a couple of minutes. That tells me that I am in a barrage of emotions during my creative process and my soul takes over - guides and all.

You will read about my friends, my childhood, my personal relationships, my wonderful dog Lloyd, my love for all animals and creatures, my hopes and fears, and my inner quests. The best part about each of these categories is that we all have them. We are all in this journey this time around, together. I believe, as deep as my soul goes, that we all live many lives. We all live on many levels of consciousness in many different planes. I also believe that animals, plants, rocks, trees, and anything of the like are equal. Everything needs to be loved and cherished. All life deserves to live free, happy, safe, devoid of any discrimination, and to be believed in. Believed in on any level they need to survive and live.

If we strive to always put ourselves first, only to accept being at the front of the line, then I'll bet we've lost sight of what we're actually standing in line for.

Just let the world around you be your guide.

I hope these words help you notice this cherished place we share.

I would like to state that my use of lower case/upper case letters and punctuation and/or lack of it in the same piece of work is intentional. I set the work onto the paper exactly as it appeared inside my head.

Peace and Go Vegan!

Ren Matney
October 2000

Contents

Blank Possibilities

This page starts out
so full of promise
and as I lay my pen down
on it's open arms I feel
like I help it
to create words and thoughts
to better itself
but
I truly am limiting it.
Any word I think of
makes that space able to only be
what that word means,
nothing more.
It is
too much to ask of me
and deep inside I know the page
is better left untouched.
Yet
I can't stop.
I hope
it will forgive me.

Forever Chant

Remove the layers of self doubt
through thoughts of
seemingly endless trials of dramatic self pity.
Touch the softness that lies still
underneath layers of
crystal clear illusion.
Cut away the 'where's' and the 'what-a-bouts'
to see what's left.
Untie your deserving pieces from
within the entanglement
of
self mutilation,
releasing them to fly again,
letting your soul float through the clouds of
wonderment and peace
ready to take on the newly
discovered world
within a state of beginner-ness
never before matched
inside this wall to wall
box to box
existence.

Sunshine Tree

Shimmering twilight bounces off branches
as if cascading into blue unknown,
all that it knows,
while swirls of memory engage as a
pass over in the eye of our sister.

White she floats always understanding.
The blossoms rotate and sway in the wind as
tiny fingers waving hello
to touch our souls, if given the chance.

Then out of the sweet scent,
soars as black as night,
a wondrous zoom of exuberance and joy,
spreading it's knowledge of love for us
to share in song.
As it's known for centuries,
their home is inside
and
their world is everywhere.
We feel the air,
we smell the scent,
we love the moon,
we envy the sky.
As I sit below I yearn to be with them
then I remind myself that
I already am.

Self Journey

If I look into my head I see
confusion trying to get out.
If I look into my heart I see
love trying to circle the bad.
If I look into my soul
I see lifetimes of searching trying to resurface.

Undying layers of old wounds
pivot throughout states of consciousness
helping us to realize
we should only look back
long enough to know
not to go searching for the paths
we traveled down uncontrollably
on the roads of our youth.
Rejoice that
we've been on those paths long enough
to see that the road ahead
is wide open
for new discovery
and self-controlled happiness.

Race Run

Circling yourself
like a comet racing 'round the universe
enables you
to only see your faults,
your likes,
your being only once every many years.

Better to engage in star-like
behavior and rest in one spot,
still able to be
a part of the universal plan
with enough
twinkle-light
to see
all the planets and their wisdom.

Then and only then
will you be truly free
to be wished upon.

Butterflies Dance

Butterflies
dance
on
extended arms
of peace.
They
are
moving
throughout
time and space
only showing up
when
you need,
be sure
and take notice.
They
deserve
at
least
that
little.

Discovery #1

Committing emotional treason
within a brain of stunted
innocence
makes a hurried perch
frantic and still.
Loosen the bind between
reality's state of
here
and
now
forever freeing thoughts
intertwined around peace
to make the future
nothing
like the past,
therefore
adding the past's lessons
into every moment of the
upcoming journey.

Un-jested Play

Around the edge of nothing
is something
and
within walls of empty
lies everything.
Move your pieces as you may
but hold loosely to them
for they are yours alone.
Fate plays the biggest hand
and
steals a peek at karma's dealt deal
before you can stone
your face.
Understand none
while learning that you
actually grieve for lost
innocence never to be found
again.
Your void is your home.
Be still.
It might hear you.

A hug

Touch me
slow me down
help me awaken from this frame
of nightmare peace.
I see only clouded thoughts
of real elemental pictures
colors fade and shady
feelings abound
throughout unrelated patterns.
Clear it up
put it down
reach a true splendid
journey.
Effortless love surrounds me
like a glove,
shielding me from the hurtful
images of pain
that try to blister my happiness.
Relax into a blissful state of joy.
No thinking.
Nor trying too hard.
Just pure essential safety
woven inside this
tapestry of love.
I breathe
and
release.

Paws

Small they are
non-greedy in their use
gentle
soft
delicate by nature
they capture my heart,
with every stroke they
make over my soul.
Yours alone are one of a kind
for they are small
by comparison to mine,
or to the ones used
by Mother Nature,
but yours alone hold enough
power and strength
to melt my heart
and crush my
insecurities.
From you they deliver nothing
but
peace.

See Through

Soft stones
are
thrown
through
nothing
windows
in hopes
of clearing
the images
we
hold
within our
mirror minds
which reflect
only
what
we think we've seen.

Front Lesson

Frozen but able to move
within a green less field
of spastic images
of the good life,
seeing everything around you
through a blind heart
makes you wonder
about love
and
the existence of any
such reality.

Ponder over tall fables
that include such deals
as happiness and self worth
as you fear the reaper
is waiting for a relaxed
moment to take you
to your fated destiny.

Outside Body

Tonight is the night it starts
whatever is set is going
to happen.
When all goes clear
and true,
you can only think safety.
Believe the testing
system and all will prevail.

Throughout the search
we all will understand.
Precise thoughts cloud
the reality set to begin.

Relax.
Let the belief just happen.

Lloyd III

Up you lift your hands and look
at me.
Help me up,
want me,
you say.
I glide my hands knowingly
around your body
and up you come.
As you turn yourself around
to find your spot I watch you,
glad you're here.
You glance at me one last time
before sitting down,
your body against mine,
your breath,
my breath.
I feel your hand on my leg.
Your chin rests against my thigh.
You give me hope.
You look at me once again.
Help me.
Want me.
I say.

Time Table

Nothing touches time,
for it must be the most
powerful piece of information
we have.
Whatever you do,
wherever you go,
time moves on.
Second by minute by hour
by day by week by month by year...
does it ever know this?
Does it care?
I'll bet time knows and does care.
Otherwise why would you feel
as if time just stood still for a moment
or flew by the other?
Time is on our side
as long as you pay attention to it.
It won't wait...
but it is your friend.

Empty Paper Box

As I blink I lose
more and more color
in the surrounded images.
Reflected in the feelings
of yesterday are
splendid light parades,
all brilliant and showy
within the prisms
of the radiant globe.
Around and around
go the feet
walking all over
my pictures
until
black and white
is all I can ever hope to see.
Sometimes I hate to think
of color anymore.
What good
is seeing the truth?
Until fate delivers
its supposed
hand,
all we have
is the thought of believing
that what it thinks
we think
it true.

Double-edge Dilemma

To love as much as needed
you must give up a lot.
Life.
Freedom.
Desires.
You must change how you
live,
or how you are
free
and what your desires become.
Not forever,
just as long as you love.

Then when fortune
takes that love
you'll think
you can be free,
you can desire.
You can live.

But will there be anything
to live for then?
to desire?
to feel free for?

Lady Blue

Within these walls
lies the undying truth
of her
she spoke
here,
she loved
here,
she gave
here,
she's still here.
I listen.
I wait for her.
Will she remember to return?
She promised.
I lie dormant within my
own flesh walls.
My bones
hold me captive
inside a prison of a living blood
cell.
A waiting person never
sleeps
or
stops.
She had better come soon.
I'm tired.

Relationship #1

I speak.
You react.
I react so you'll speak.
We get nowhere.

I stop feeling.
You start.
I give in and trust.
You stop and disappear.
We get nowhere.

I listen.
You forget.
I decide to forget.
You remember.
We get nowhere.

I love you.
I hate me.
You get nowhere.

You love me.
You hate me.
I get nowhere.

I love you.
I love you, too.
We get nowhere.

Reality

Deny all the dream features
that arise within
waking moments,
for unrealistic possibilities
can torment a desiring mind.
Choose not to follow
after time,
it seems the only undying
length of hope to cling to.
Disappointment,
take it within
each different stride.
For the end result is always
the same within a
taught frame of mind.
Withstanding life-killing events
makes us numb
to the pain
we actually
cause ourselves
without knowing.

Tree-dom Rings

Inside the bark
a world thrives to create
a feeling of peace
and harmony
to spill out in leafy hands
and tangy drops of
fruit filled love.
How sweet this colony
breeds existence for
so many.

We all are one.
That group,
this pack,
all together.

We need the cooperation
of all workers
within each tree,
each house,
each building,
each mountain.

Peace will arise.

Too Much

Pushed,
shoved aside
from my own life
by me.
How can I live with that?
I am only where
I
let myself get.
Why am I here?
Why am I in control?
I shouldn't be.
Tell me what to say.
Tell me what to think.
Tell me what.
What I did.
What I do.
Then help me rewrite
the ending.
I don't like the way
I think
it's going to end.

Pity Rain

Really relaxed,
totally at peace,
pushing at easy thoughts,
making them
nuances of ecstasy
abound within my spirit
named a goal.
Withstand, withhold,
without I am sorrow
and I fill empty
gutters of strangers' homes
overflowing with victim pity.
Ugly is the clog of my
supposed reality.

White Angel

When I look at you I think to myself
how can I help you?
What can I do for you?
Tell me where it hurts.
Show me where your pain is.
I'll eat it.
I'll throw it out.
I wish I could pick you up so high
I could set you on a star
and keep you from harm or sickness.
You would float around on that star
smiling and laughing
until forever.
Your eyes hold the universe
so within its arms is where
you belong.
I got to borrow you for awhile.
I will never be the same.
You breath is my breath.
You eyes became my eyes.
You gave me love
and I couldn't even save you.

Tidal Waves

I'm happy until I think
about it.
I can be ready for anything
until it's here.
I stand up for all
if there is no chair near.
Thoughts inside my head are
pure until they form conscious
words.
I smile until I see it.
I laugh until I hear it.
I love until I feel it.
Then I'm afraid
and I hide
until I'm found.
Them I'm happy...

until I think about it.

Easter Chair

A wise man lay inside his bed
He looks at me with eyes full of love
so much that I can feel
it surround me and caress me
like tiny fingers making my whole body tingle.
He smiles.
That takes most of his energy alone
but he doesn't care,
He cries
which takes no energy,
for they are uncontrollable tears of truth.
Holding my hand he says
'don't be anxious and I love you' then he dies.
His comment of love makes me wonder
Will I miss him too much?
Will I ever love like he said?
Will I need things?
Does he already know?
If I let him down
I will weep for the selfish act I am doing.
He deserves better. He made me promise.
Why do the great ones get taken?
Or would they tell you
that we think they are great only because
they are leaving and now know the truth?
Either way it's still up to us to remember
and I will never forget.

Grasslands

I close my eyes
and I see wheat fields of gold.
Within it
are the dreams,
of my future,
all the wishes I ever made
upon a first star of the twilight
held inside each stalk of pure
golden life.
My wishes are safe there.
I trust the wheat
and the wheat
trusts me.
Together we sway in the summer breeze
full of strength,
never bending
lest we break.
No fear.
We bury into the rich earth
and are reborn,
wishes and all.
For true trust, true beauty and
true wishes never end.
I shut my eyes and drift off,
thought in thought with the
wheat fields.

Morning Thought

Seldom seen
a day so wonderful
that holds so much beauty.
The sky twinkles inside
the loving arms that beam
out from the rising sun
as my love for you
grows and grows.
Let's make memories today,
the kind only
dreams can make.

Different Animals

Tugging at the empty heart strings
of the enemy,
we cling to hope that they will
see.
Notice the faces, we scream.
Glance at the souls if
only for a moment
and maybe you'll figure out
that you're playing a God role
you haven't the mental skill to
interpret.
Compassion is something we all
deserve.
God will get you, you scream.
You're born of evil, you cry.
Less than you, in your eyes,
means you get to kill us?
Or them?
We cry peace.
You cry death.
And the Gods
just cry.

Wipe Clean

Stop making me have no choice but to say
I hate you and I hate what you've
become.
You stop hearing me when I speak,
you say
you listen to me but you see me
speaking
and you only hear yourself.
I have no ties to you.
I have nothing to owe you.
You are here only for seconds,
so listen only to you.
I don't care
but
I hate you no more.
Now I don't even care enough to hate.

Let Go

If I'm only allowed to do
what you want,
when you want,
like you want,
then you want yourself
not me.
Because me is going to only know
how to do things like me
and
when it's right for me.
I can learn
but be patient with me
because I need to see you,
I need to understand you.
Then if it's right for me
I will try.
If not then okay,
it's your problem
and my beating drum
shall go on
and on.

Splendor Field

A quiet majestic breath
falls over the land
as tiny dew drops form over its waking
body
creating a blanket of warmth
with the power of the universe
wrapped up inside
each brilliantly shining
droplet.
The hush is stillness.
Its peaceful splendor captures
our hearts,
our minds,
and stalls them into
overview.
Contentment emerges.
Live within this rapture
with each wakeful step
you now take
for you are moving
into oneness
with the mother earth,
with the eternal universe,
with the inhabitants of all we know
and of all we don't.
Become what it wants.
Become your own tiny gentle
droplet of peace.

Reality Point

When you touch the blue spirit
all life engulfs around your head,
speaking in tongues
to a voice that can no longer hear.
Circle the choice, you ponder
Is it right?
Is it wrong?
Am I touching pure essence
or leaving my bloody trail
behind for you to see?
Gallop through the sounds of
the ocean,
float around the sun
like gulls upon the breath
of the Gods and Goddesses.
They blink within the rays
of the moon and
their
love answers you
in
giant beams of
stoic virtue.

Please Believe

Looking around at people
I feel their
energy so strongly at times
that I think
I could just explode,
not out of anger
but from pure
longing for happiness.

Before and After

Touch the dove of everlasting
peace
and forever be in a realm of
sorrow,
for it is not until after
you have
witnessed pure serenity
that you can feel
any pain.
Before, the fateful grasp
your soul
knew no different
than what was
honest and true.
Remember that
and you have
a chance.

Motorme

All the energies of the universe
encompass turning wheels of emotion.
Within my inner self all
external forces ride.
I am ultimately produced
throughout these energies.
They create me.
They feed my strengthening hunger,
churning and churning
they notice the wrongs of
this impetuous dimension
throughout my run
inside the shell of this
life.
I desire to feel the emotions
strongly enough to carry me on to
brighter and more luminous
chances of fate.

Yellow Light

While turning the wheel
of blissful contentment,
I somehow end up traveling
down a road I do not
understand.
I think I'll put myself in
neutral for a bit
to let the feelings of
true self and
eternal honesty
ride the waves
of my soul,
thus
driving me into
who I really am,
away from all the
charted streets and
into peaceful uncharted
engagements.

Don't Go

Do I cover you up so
you are safe or so I am
safe?
Do you hide to save me
or
to save yourself?
When I hold you, am I?
Or
are you actually holding me?
If I touch you is it
for me
or
is it for you?
When you kiss me
who is it for?
When we sit together,
who sits by whom?
When you leave
will I get to go too
or is it just you?
I don't ever want to know,
do you?

Rape of a Lifetime

For i am small,
i don't know.
You ask me a question
when you really don't want
my answer that i am
too young to give;
my innocent and new
mind can't even get to a place
where an answer will form,
for i am small
and i don't understand the thought
you pose in front of me.
You play games with my
soul like it is the toy
you hold out in front of your
filthy game.
Pose me and make me your
little secret and give me
my consolation prize as a
lock and take the key to my
life to keep me sealed with
hidden misunderstanding,
for I am now even smaller
and I still don't know.

Little Black Worlds

Eyes so deep
I can hear the ocean
of thought
and
of dreams.
All knowledge is inside
the colors of natural love,
browns and blacks and whites
encompass the understanding
you pour into my soul
with one glance.
Look at me here,
follow me with your gaze
over there.
For I cannot live
without your unconditional stare
piercing my being
and making me overflow
with our love.

I only hope my eyes do the same.

Had Enough

It really makes me wonder
why people don't think.
You speak. You hurt.
You listen, don't you?
My voice wounds are bleeding.
You speak more,
still not thinking.
You speak. You crash down spirits.
You listen? No more.
I say.
Why waste my seconds on
hearing you not listen.
You not hearing is loud.
You speaking has become very quiet.
Shhh...I can see you,
but I hear nothing.
You say nothing. I start to heal.
My voice wounds stop hurting.
I stay scared but I can control my pain now.
I listen loud to you,
saying nothing
and yet I hear voices,
my voices,
saying...your seconds wasted on not thinking
have nothing to do with me anymore.
I smile.

So...

so small you sit
perched up on your cloud,
you see all.
so innocent you view the
goings on
with no judgment.
so gentle in your wants and
in your desires,
all you need is love.
so fragile your heart,
carry me into the horizon
with your kisses
until
all I see is our two beings breathing
as one.
so small you sit
up on your cloud,
wait for me...

Do I really?

Why do I care?
I really don't
I'm totally free,
I'm rolling with it all.
Yet before I know it
I've cared
and then all my energy
goes into something
I actually don't
care at all about.
Why do I even care.
I really don't.

Park Bench

An old woman sits by herself
surrounded with memories of
the past,
past loves,
past joys,
past forever's.
Move over on the bench so
the ghosts of yesterday
and the spirits of tomorrow
can sit next to her
and glide her into peace.
See her smile?

She knows this already.

Hidden

Perched in the branches that
I flattened like a nest
I would watch the world go by.

Hidden from peering eyes
no longer human,
at least
in my mind,
free to be...I was then.
See what I want,
hear what I want.
One with nature and
involved with the beasts
around me.
Why was I so young?

Now as an adult,
I still sit in my nest
and watch,
still looking,
only now I can't
choose what I see or hear.

Purpose

As a child I would wonder
what was out there.
I could feel it,
I could tell it was there,
I just couldn't see it or find it.
Now
I keep looking,
keep wondering
have I found it yet?
I still can't see it.

I wonder...
am I still supposed to be looking?

The Flower

With brightly colored fingers,
shades of life are spread
throughout each other to
shine with the sun,
to point
our souls to the sky
and revel in your majestic scent.
We can see you,
wild
or
purposeful,
you are all necessary.
Light our world with
your innocence and ignite
our lives with
all the colors and the shades
you can become.
Reminding us that
we too,
are just the same.

Simple Truth

A drum is only a drum if you beat it.
A smile is only a smile if you didn't plan it.
A happy thought is only a happy thought
if you didn't mean to think it.
Anger is only anger when you don't
think about it first.
Touching somebody is only touching someone
if both reach out.
Seeing the sunset is only seeing the sunset
if the birds fly off into it.
Rain is only rain if you take the time to feel it.
Friends are only friends if you didn't
set out to find them.
Hearing the wolf cry is only a wolf crying if it
made you stop dead in your tracks.
Feeling a hummingbird fly by your face
is only a hummingbird flying by
if it took your breath away.
See?
Simple, isn't it?

Stop Me

If I could shut down
I think I'd be happier.
But you can't shut down,
at least not completely.
Parts of you keep working.
Your heart.
Your breath.
Your mind.
They push on through whatever the
situation your body wants to stop
being a part of.
Is this wise?
Is that a good request?
I think probably not.
Trust your insides,
for your body is a shell
working and revealing your
true inner self.
Keep that journey on
strong.

Overwhelmed

The stars are out.
When I look up at them
I feel one with the universe.
It hurts me not to be able
to reach out and touch them.
Even more not to be able to
look up and understand them.
I don't understand stuff
here.
Why can't I look up and understand?
To be able to understand at least
one part would be great.
However not to understand
the stars
makes me love
them more.
That's why I love.

Partner

Could I walk your path if given the chance?
Would you let me?
Would you want me to?
As I sit under the sky in the fields
of my thoughts I wonder what you see.
Are you looking?
If I sit quietly enough I can
hear the clouds moving overhead
creating the music I walk to.

I walk down a path to you,
but find nothing.
You are gone and I am alone.
So I sit back down. I wonder,
should I follow?
Is this my chance?
Could I walk your path to find
you?

Truth

I'm not here to make your
life better,
I'm here for my life.
If our paths cross and we like it,
fine.
But don't make me in control
of your happiness and then
never let me guide you.
Better I stay
to
myself.

Piglets

i feel your pain
so deep within my soul
i have trouble going on.
Why can't i stop it?
Why do i feel it?
Why should you?
i am sorry.
You are beautiful.
You deserve everything good.
i feel your anguish.
i want you to know.
i hope it helps.
i hope i can.

Two Deer Forum

Feeling power within
overturns mountains
of guilt,
removing all doubts
that true ecstasy exists.
Gentle beings safely
peer into the darkness
pierced with our
wondrous streams
of lit love.
Silvered swans
I've carried over to the light
hide and seek for me here
in their place of enchantment.
Sound waves trek over my heart
until eclipsing metaphors
circle my wordless brain,
numbing my senses
to the enchanted,
thankful heart.
Teach me to be naturally me,
as naturally as
you are you,
roaming inside
your realm of peace.

The Trees

I used to become one with the tree.
I was a child but when I took
that first step up into the escape
I would gain the power of
these quiet giants.
Up, up I'd go, leaving the world
behind.
Entering my own sight-seeing world,
out I'd look,
seeing my own life.
I was one with the wind.
I could feel the tree entering my
soul.
The child would disappear,
I would take flight,
soaring through the images
of my own imagination,
not ever being the kid who climbed
up,
wishing never to have to climb
down,
for then I was free.

Clouds

I think clouds are the
shadows of past or other dimensions of life.
Look into them.
What do you see?
They are too powerful to be
just clouds.
If you look and see something,
remark on what you see.
For it could be trying to tell you
or remind you of something.
Take pleasure with positive energy
that they are our guides,
taking us through this journey
not alone
and not so unaware.
Makes a cloudy day enchanting
doesn't it?

Birds

Your rainbow branches
guide you to me
out from the rays of warmth,
love is why you soar,
bringing your song to awaken my being.
Calm flies in
whenever you are near.
Floating over the sea
is where
you take my soul.
How lovely for you to remove me
from this place.
Even if only for a moment.

I'll be First

I'll start today.
Today I'll be the first to listen.
No longer will I need to be
the one talking.
Unimportant are my thoughts
for they usually cause too much
confusion and mostly
for me.
I'll act with compassion.
I'll see like a newborn
learning about the peace this
life can bring.
I'll move through today like
a new fawn taking its first
steps in the great forest
of life.
Don't know what's around the
bend but I'll face it with
tranquil peace.

I promise.

Jill Untitled

You are a brightly shining star.
Illuminate through all your province.
All who gaze above just
long enough
will be awed with your essence.
Their justified placement,
their feelings of belonging and worth,
will be enhanced
with your noble energy.
It sends the greatly effortless universe
into spirals of peaceful bliss.
Touch all you can,
for your essential heart
cares for what
most eyes
don't see.

Just a Thought

How can one be so selfish
that eating another's flesh
is only considered bad
if the flesh comes from one
who's
just like you?

Life Question

Sometimes I think I know,
then I try
and
fail.
That scares me away
from wanting to know
what I didn't in the first place.
What if the new knowledge
makes me feel
for that
instant
I can do all
only
then to fail again?
Is new knowledge worth
that risk?

O'Cow

Quiet eyes that rest inside
your gentle head.
Why must they be so sad
looking?
You are a magnificent being
full of special gifts
one should share.
You have love,
respect,
joy
inside you.
Why must you be killed?
Why can't people see those inside,
instead of just a beauty's life being
turned into a slaughtered lunch?
I'll love you for what you are.
I only wish
that
it were enough to save you
from your given placement of misery.

Thoughts

I see you best when
my eyes are closed.
I hear you best when
my ears stop listening.
I know you best
when I say nice to
meet you.
I love you most
when I stop thinking...

Eaten Animals

I sought afternoons
that were filled with
peace and serenity.
Instead I found
different.
It makes me drop inside
like a condensation
from the highest point
when thoughts of you
being hurt fill my soul.
Wasted.
Unloved.
Un-noticed.
Who is cold enough
inside to not see you?
To not hear you take a breath?
Like them.
Just the same.
You too want your share of love and life.
I can't fathom
why people
don't see.
I see.
I love you.
I'm trying to save you.

Building Blocks

Sitting, waiting for my memories
to
stop
unleashes
pain underlining
my worry.
To touch the inside part of your foundation
requires
tools much too fragile to misuse.
Reshaping your walls
into rooms of understanding
regulates the pressure
to be just the perfect
color.
Allow your self-house
to move and change
shape,
otherwise
what kind of home can it be?

Rabid Reality

Sitting.

Waiting.

For you to not see me.

It's okay.

You only see when you want.

When I see you look away,

it kills me.

Lost Time

When the realm of uncontrolled views,
that have been unearthed by forces deep
within teachings of survival clears like the
soft delicate nature of a freshly bloomed rose,
it captures my right reality.
Inside, my inner tone sings once again.
Walls of brick, layered so thick and deep,
dissipate my reaching up for help
from the well of despair
in which I am trapped clear at the bottom,
feet securely fastened by the self doubt,
clogged up with weakness
within a head of dreams unvoiced.
I bloom once again as if from a dream.
Where did the lost time go?
I do not remember all of which I didn't say,
nor all of what I wanted to think.
Save me.
Sometimes I feel the walls closing in on me
within an instant,
always reminding me that for now, at least,
the well, being a pit,
is a scheduled fate.
It is returning and I am unable to know
when or where.
I ask again. Save me.
But whom am I asking and
what is to be saved from?

Good Boy

It's too hard.
I can't try anymore.
Don't make me talk.
Don't make me fall,
but if I do
catch only the parts you like
then mold me into what it is
you desire
and then add the strings.
I'll move when you want.
You'll be happy.
I'll speak when you
are the voice.
You'll be secure.
I'll go where
you manipulate the tether of my life
within your bored grasp.
You'd never be alone.
Leave me in a box with the lid shut tight,
when you go.
Open me up and take me out
until you go away again.
I'll be your toy so long as you're happy.
If you're not, cut the strings
letting me fall into a heap
and finally do the deciding
about
me.

Too Usual

One track mind
One track...
one...
what?
One track mind.
How empty that must feel.
All that false filling inside?
You don't know.
You don't understand.
You don't think.
You don't stay.
You don't want to listen.
You don't talk back.
You don't help.

Shut up and save me from my thoughts.

For they hurt me more than you.

Self Titled

Trapped.
I am within a realm
that I have never seen before.
Always knew it was coming
but so soon
or
are you overdue?
No sentences finish
nor any thoughts that arise
to a blissful state.
Only mixed up phrases
spelling the path you have
created for me with all my help and guidance.
You are confusion. You want confession.
You make me die inside
each time you
whisper sweet nothings
into my soul.
Try. Think. Speak.
You're right.
You're in the right way.
I hate you.
Although not really.
'Cause I don't even know what you are.

Trapped.

Questions.

Ask.

Answers.

Get nothing.

Ask.

Answer.

Never ask again.

Little White Angel

Here you sit, soft next to my side.
I feel your breath in and out of your being
reminding me that you are still here.
You didn't leave me, it wasn't time.
There is time for everything, so someone said.
I do believe this to be true.
Our time now is to love.
We need you. We need you always.
Your glance pierces our souls with
the beauty your eyes hold.
Wise and full of wonderment, you make us see
the familiar as new.
Within your smile is held the eternal key to our
peace. Sit next to me until forever.
For this is honest silence and
you connecting with me is pure freedom
to soar through the heavens together.
Our moment has been extended,
we must not waste it.
So home we shall go, back to what you know.
We must share it and notice it,
cherish it and see what a wonderful gift
our absolutely blissful little family really is.
No complaints, no faults, no worries,
just happiness and love.
I believe you know this already and you are
teaching us that gift.
Thank you, little white angel.

Faith 101-102

Miraculous images throughout
my empathy engage the test
of the Gods to try and
clear a path to save you.

It is a confusing road to travel when you
trust the Gods and Goddesses
but you don't trust yourself.
If you don't trust in yourself
then how can you honestly trust another?

Entangled Fancy

Circling the harvest moon
a feather
floats alone.
It doesn't realize its power.
It doesn't know
its worth.
Does it remember its days
of projecting nature upon
its light and heavenly true host?
Now should it wonder
where it's going
or why it's been sent?
I look for this feather
to free me inside my loyal
limited boundaries,
to learn
to escape my float-less range.
To fly free on the winds of life
we are drifting
forever.

Ball Glass

A childlike innocence follows
where the small space travels,
floating through a melancholy act,
feeling as if she could float
right above the colorful and almighty heavens.
If one has the childlike innocence
to float above the heavens
then one can reveal the
true reason for their
plight on this fanciful,
rolling and turning
sphere.

Wish

Touch me with your glossy clear space,
remove my thoughts one by one
until I can only think for myself.
I'll turn over and over
within the realm of consciousness throughout
my journey, hoping that with each step
I slip into every star's grasp
filling my soul with your energy so it overflows
and I can reach all and share inner peace.
Within that state of pure awe you can't breathe,
you don't even want to.
No thoughts register and that's fine.
Images float around your head,
circling your body with tingles abounding,
reminding you that for this moment you are still
alive. Pleasure so awesome you think time
must be standing beside you, quiet and still.
Is this truth really happening? Remind yourself
that it is and that you deserve it. Smile.
For dreams like this do come true.

Questioned Control

It takes away my thoughts of clear vision,
It takes away my hunger,
It takes away my desire,
It takes away my voice,
It takes away my strength,
It takes away my breath,
It takes away my emotions,
It takes away my hearing,
It takes away my likes and dislikes,
It takes away my hopes and my dreams,
It takes away my fears.

Except one.

I fear I don't know what it is.

Instant Fixings

The center cries for forgiveness
as the edges fight to claw
away the layers of abusive
corrosion.
Discoloring face
Cringe into a heap as thoughts
and un-done worthless deeds
go forever on
as less-than-goods
and
never-good-enough's.
Remind yourself
it could always be worse or it
could seem that way.
Believe it or not
things are never what they are.

Caught

Stop telling me to have a nice day
when you only think of your day
and only see your self,
and only hear your voice
and all its non-thinking gibberish.
Why am I wasting my time listening to you
suck up to yourself
only to waste my own time
re-thinking why you do what you do?
It's me who's wrong.
Only not why you think
but because I took the time to
expect you to care.

Debbie

You are a wondrous sight
building on a foundation of love.
Your giving's make friendship real.
Sincerity beams from your wise
yet beginning eyes
ready to share truth,
open to learn more.
Hearts abound throughout
your life-lines as they
pump the river of existence
within your being,
carrying all your love
inside and out.
A hug so strong you
could bet your soul on it's
sincerity.
For she is true.
she is honest.
She is the universe's most
awesomely beautiful creation...
a true friend.

Bars

Insinuating breaths of conciseness
expel charges of deviant behavior,
rebel against feelings of inadequacy
and punch your forces through
to the bright neon fortress
displayed on the other side.
Refuge is sought and momentary
safety is condensed
inside a reassuring lust
for now being called love,
for it is a bond near any soul
trying to crackle into
spit-on phases of sin.
It is real,
if only for a moment.
Icy shades of reality
break out the colorful light chambers
who called you out of the night hiding.
Thicken your skin.
Walk with your head low.
Don't make eye contact and wait
for the dark safety to return.

Dim Light

Lost in the light,
I search for a place,
see me in the shadows?
I am the same color.
I am lost, you find me
even if only for a brief moment
and I feel safe love at last.
Back to the daylight
I hide,
staying blended with the shadows.
Here comes another,
wide eyed and lost.
Will you help me tonight?
I wish I would be found.

Trunk Down

I touch softness with the essential bark
of the nearest tree, its roughness,
its common branches, escalate my inner
knowledge, to finger out into the skies,
to grasp the truths I have yet to imagine.
Rooted within fences without gates,
they turn and turn with no escape.
Leap and bound and run so to sit up
and perch one endless ponder of universal
thought. Each leaf holds the veins of yesterday
that fall to the ground of today.
Touch it, feel it, drop yourself down
and finally live.

Problem Solved

The failsafe blackness surrounds
the entity full of wanting and trust,
swallowing eternal souls in one quick breath.
No hope of a last chance to run around looking,
guessing, speaking into pain.
Why should all words create?
Can't they just tell the story, the verse?
I do know the voice that is the ending of this
despair. It is not the eternal blackness
once thought,
nor the rays of the shiny heat.
It can't be found in thought
or words or deeds
if it's empty.

Then just do nothing
and all will be fine.

Dejection Up

Whether to give up focus or not
seems to be the question everyone asks.
Whether to re-focus or not is the question
people should ask.
Touching the surface of intellectual thought
makes for eternal manifestations of derived,
misplaced care. Hold on to it.
Don't give it away, for it seems never to
get back to you the same.
Only let people borrow the portions you see fit.
Then when they give you back what was
yours in the first place,
it's still the same as what you gave.
No more,
no less,
no change,
no matter what they saw it to be.
It's yours to focus on again and again.

A.M.

Here I sit
wondering why,
how does it happen?
When does it begin?
I tell myself not to,
I hope you wont,
then you do.
And I did.
When love is what brought
us together,
how can it tear us up?
I'm not done with you.
We are not finished,
just a bit off.
We need to get on the
same path again.
Here I sit
wondering how.

Channeled Wisdom

Sweet truth
evolves out of empty
un-understanding.
We rotate
around the rocks
of presence
as if the harder we feel,
the less we are.

Paths of forked
knowledge allow us to
choose our destiny
and control the outcome,
any way we choose.

Heed wisdom that
un-choosing
is the best road to find
true self.

Always
believe in
spontaneous
walking.

Glimmer

Even the smallest hope makes the world look
better. Trees are bigger,
sun is brighter,
warmer, colder.
Smells are different
not just quickly pass
but linger and formulate.
It's glorious.
The breeze enters every pore
and stays inside you
as changes within your soul
float to the surface.
You breathe for the first time,
the ground has never felt stronger,
more solid, like you are finally
sure-footed and safe.

Remember,
it all began with
just a bit of hope.

For additional copies of this book by mail
order and/or other works by this author
please contact:

otherechoes@cs.com